Broken But Okay

Rev. Dr. Walter J. Green

Published in 2018 in the United States by Donna Cox Ministries, a subsidiary of Personal Best Ministries LLC, Xenia, OH 45485

Library of Congress Cataloging-in-Publications Data
Green, Walter J.

I Am Broken: But I'm Okay And So Are You/Walter J. Green
ISBN 978-0-9796955-7-5
Includes scriptures (Holy Bible)
All scriptures are taken from the Holy Bible, New Century Version®. Copyright © 2005 by Thomas Nelson, Inc.

Summary: Life struggles equip us for the next phase of our journey. This book teaches readers that it is ok to be broken because, through brokenness, God equips people to do greater works for His kingdom.

A 2018 publication of
Donna Cox Ministries/PBM Press
A subsidiary of

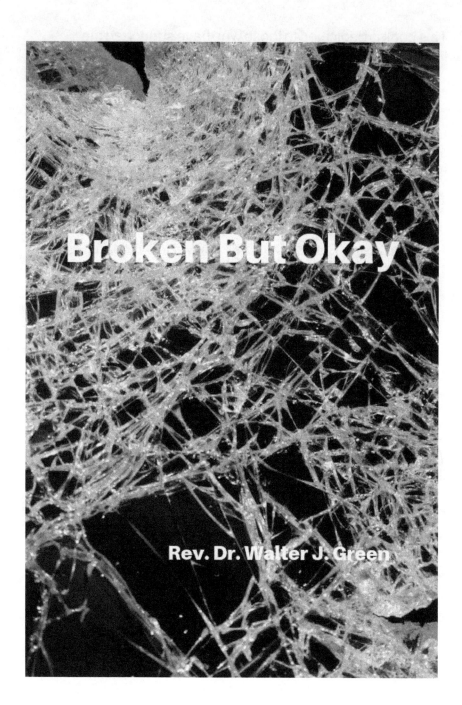

Broken But Okay

Rev. Dr. Walter J. Green

This book is dedicated to those who have supported me throughout my ministry journey:

♥ my wife, Sara;

♥ my daughters, Lynne Elizabeth, Janaye Alexandria Lynne, and Jadelynne Jeanine Marie;

♥ my mother, Gayle Lee Green;

♥ my brothers, Matthew, Michael and Duane

♥ my sisters, Madonna and LaTonya

♥ Nazarene Baptist Church Family, New Orleans, LA; Christian Unity Baptist Church Family, New Orleans, LA;

♥ Omega Baptist Church Family, Dayton, OH;

♥ Mt Calvary Christian Church Family, Dayton, OH;

♥ Friendship Baptist Church Family, Memphis, TN and

♥ To the memory of my youngest brother, Wallace Anthony Green

With Gratitude, I thank Rev. Dr. Donna M. Cox for loving me through this project, and for giving more guidance than words can express. Thank you for being a sister, friend, editor, publisher, and mentor.

Table of Contents

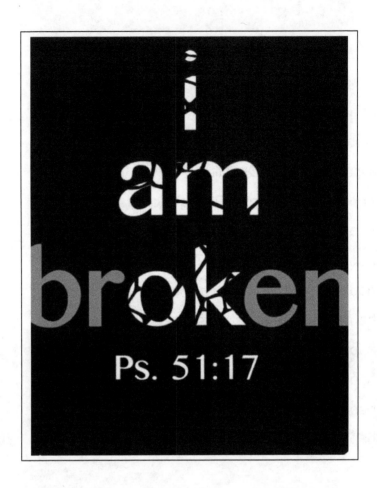

The sacrifices of God are a broken spirit;
a broken and contrite heart,
O God, you will not despise.

Preface

Many people who serve in ministry have placed themselves under the pressure to perform to unrealistic expectations. This pressure alone affects their health, family relationships, and their position in the overall community. The need to be perfect, the need to be the best at one's craft, is the order of the day. However, when this is not your reality, what do you do?

As a result of being in the rat-race to perform and compete against a worldly system of success, we often miss the need to honor the voice of God as He speaks to our lives. The toxicity of performance-based ministry often makes us miss what matters most, so we are left with many casualties. It is so important to remind people who serve in ministry that we are servants of God. We are seeking to become more like Him. It is not that we have achieved, but every day we are moving closer to being what He has called us to be.

Like the clay before the potter, God is shaping us into a worthy vessel. Our challenge is learning to love ourselves, our families, our congregations, and our communities. We also must recognize that love is always developing and never complete. It does not yet appear what we shall be if we continue to honor and follow the Word of God, and be led by the Holy Spirit. Our ministries are stories that are unfolding, not books with a final chapter.

We are being shaped by our imperfections, struggles, let-downs, failures, and mistakes. We are not finished products but people who are becoming. When we lose focus of the fact that we are becoming, we become increasingly frustrated, overwhelmed, and begin to burn out. This leads to moral failures, abuse of the ministry, and isolation.

Knowing that I do not have it altogether and recognizing my humanity, reminds me to rely on God for direction and fulfillment. I am grateful for those who struggle with me in my brokenness to become what God has destined for me to become.

I could never become what or who God destined for my life without the community that surrounds me in this journey.

Introduction

Failure is a part of everyone's life. It can be manifested through pain, frustration, fear, and in many other ways. Mothers, fathers, sisters, brothers, husbands, wives, doctors, lawyers, teachers, engineers, law enforcement personnel, and even pastors, all experience, live through, and struggles with failure. For some, it may have been the end of a marriage, or the termination of a job. It could have been the result of the losing a major contract. Failure can show up in so many different ways but it is common to every living person. Are we less than a whole person because we did not get it right? Are our lives not worth living because we failed in marriage, in our career, or the last project we undertook? Too often we find ourselves wondering because we did not meet some external expectation of success.

We live in a world that celebrates our success and not our failures. A world where we live with shame as a result of not getting it right, or not having it all together. We struggle with not getting the recipe right, not passing the exam, or not knowing the right path to take. In this life, we get no credit for trying, or for being in the race. We are not rewarded for the pain or the disappointment. The attributes of failure lead to frustration that causes us to be broken.

The world tends to only celebrate getting it right, and not the fact that we were in the race. Think for a minute. Who was the second-place team in the Super Bowl two years ago? What presidential candidate ran against the current president? We have missed the fact that we are on a journey of becoming. We are seeking to become the best person we can be. In becoming, we must travel down paths that challenge who we are and help us in building character.

This book is about a life journey filled with being broken, and recognizing that in being broken we learn to grow. Brokenness can lead us to get better. As result of brokenness, we learn to improve on things if we do not give up. We must learn how to keep working despite what it looks like. Too often we quit because we did not get right. We throw in the towel because it was too hard to overcome the pain of failure.

All of us have the marks of failure on our lives. We bear the wounds of frustration and disappointment. It is no different from a mother who feels guilty because of the moral failures in her life. It is the same for the committed and caring doctor who used the best medical techniques known to humanity, but his patient still expired. Additionally, the lawyer who put in many hours to defend a client only to have a jury come back with a guilty verdict. Disappointment, frustration, and pain are not limited to just some of us. We all will meet with these feelings within the course of our lives.

Even those of us who help others deal with failure and disappointment in their lives, will find ourselves facing the same challenges. These failures leave us feeling broken. Brokenness is not limited to one group, one profession, or one social economic group. Brokenness is not a female issue or a male issue. It is an issue that all humans face in their journey. Brokenness is real and shows up in the life of all. Our challenge is learning how to be ok with being broken.

Chapter 1
The Question

I remember that lazy afternoon while I sat watching television. My wife asked me a question that haunted me. The question, although simple, was complex. She simply asked, "Are you happy?" Not sure of what she was asking, I responded, "What do you mean?" She said, "You do not have the same excitement that you once exhibited?"

She continued to ask me the following questions: Do you like what you are doing? Are you getting tired of the ministry or the people you serve?

Serious reflection was in order after my wife's questions daunted me for a few days. Her questions had me wondering what I looked like in her eyes? More importantly, what was I looking like before others? What was I doing or not doing that would cause her to ask such these questions?

As far as I was concerned, I was the go-to person, but my life told a different story. I was broken and did not know it. I was stressed out and was morbidly overweight. As a result of living in this personal chaos, I found myself having open heart surgery to repair a mitral valve. Complications kept me in the hospital for a month. For two weeks I was in an induced coma because the medical staff could not wean me off the ventilation machine. After a staph infection and other complications, the grace of God brought me through the worst medical ordeal of my life. Never would I have thought that I would die, but I promised myself that I did not want to be in that position ever again in my life.

I was living an exhausting life that was out of control. It all hit me when the surgeon came to talk with me the day before surgery. He asked, "What do you do for a living." I responded,

"I am a pastor." He said, "That explains it!" He went on to say, "You have the heart of an eighty-year-old person." I was 42 years old, but the life I was living was taking a toll on my heart. He also shared with me that stress was killing me. After he left the room, I sat in silence, thinking about what I had just heard from the man who would do the surgery to repair the valve in my heart. Stress was killing me.

I was guilty of not doing the very things that I had counseled so many people to do. I had talked with many people about living a life out of control. I had talked with people about priorities and understanding their limitations. I had counseled men and women to learn to release worry, anxiety, and stress from their lives. I was the one talking to people about the need to rest, learning to be ok with not being perfect, and living the best life possible. However, I was guilty of not finding release and respite for myself.

Many pastors have difficulty admitting that we are broken, and we do not have our lives all together. Pastors counsel everyone how to have healthy spiritual lives, but way too often we ignore our own personal and spiritual lives. Pastors seek to lead others to find peace and rest, but rarely come to grip with the fact that we also need to learn how to rest. God rested on the seventh day. Are people in ministry greater than God?

I did not know what true peace was. I did not know how to be still. I was, as Joyce Meyers the televangelist, would call, "a victim of Approval Addiction." I believed the more hours and the harder I worked, the greater the success I could expect. Yes, there was always something to do, but I was not always effective in the doing. Not only was I sometimes ineffective, I was killing myself, and doing it in the name of God, faith, ministry, the church, family, community, and civic responsibility. The truth is I was doing it because I was afraid of failure. I wanted to be successful in ministry, community work, personal faith, and above all, family. I could not see that stress and the workload did not make me successful. Instead, it was leading to my demise. I was broken and did not realize it.

The surgery and near-death experience forced me to make changes. But they were not lasting. A decade later, I found myself back in the same trap that led to a place I promised I would never return. My wife's question triggered a time of critical self-reflection, a reality check. I wanted to believe that I had gotten it together, but what I was believing was not my true reality.

My life was filled with a whole lot of stuff. I had demands from everyone, the church, other pastors, community people, family, and friends. People were depending on me for advice, to teach, to lead, to share, and be present. I realize that I was doing it all over again ten years later. I was bewildered because I had friends that I saw lose their families, turn to alcohol, experience moral failures, walk away from ministry, and I still did not get it. I counseled with many of them, prayed for their families, and ministries. I cried with fellow ministers and shared in their pain, but I still did not understand my personal brokenness. Maybe I thought I was invincible. Maybe I thought I could handle it all. Maybe I thought it would not happen to me. I now realize I was broken by the very things that I thought would give me the greatest joy. I was broken by chasing life. My life was out of control because I never took time to experience and truly *live* life. I was broken by pressure to perform and I was not present in the performance. I had a great story, but I did not have a great life.

The scary part of this journey is that I could see the struggle in others, but I could not see it in myself. I had become a hoarder of "next," the next workshop, the next position, the next assignment, the next level. I became a victim of blaming myself when it did not work. I would barrage myself with questions. "Did I do enough?" "Did I study or prepare hard enough?" "Did I look hard enough?" I was filled with questions and not a sufficient amount of answers, or answers I was ready to accept. I am learning that you can have all the right tools and methods and still not know how to maneuver through life. I am learning that you can teach others how to use the tools in their lives, but if you are not taking advantage of the knowledge you so freely share, you might as well not know it.

My wife was always reminding me, you can teach how to live a good life, but can you live it? I refuse to die because of living a reckless life that is out of control while trying to help others get their lives in control. I am still haunted by that simple question my wife asked me, "Are you happy?"

I wear a lot of hats: pastor, husband, father, son, brother, cousin, friend, volunteer, instructor, administrator, counselor, advisor, board member, president, vice president, the list goes on. Yet, in all I do, am I happy? Am I happy with the quality of the relationships I have? Am I happy with my relationship with God? Am I happy with myself? Am I happy with the relationship my wife and I have? Am I satisfied with the relationship I am developing with my family? Is the ministry satisfying? When I look deep into my heart, am I truly happy? And if I'm not, what am I going to do about it?

The challenge is one of finding myself and not defining myself. I did not need to know who I was. I needed to know where I was. I needed to be reminded of my calling. I knew my position, but I did not know where I was, so I kept searching, and seeking to be in a place where I had already arrived. I was unaware of my location. Too often we are trying to escape the place that we prayed for, and worked hard to be in. In that place we must learn to blossom, to grow, and to appreciate.

One of greatest challenges for many of us is to recognize our brokenness. Brokenness is not about looking at the damage of our lives. It's about seeing the places of growth and development. Too often, we see brokenness as a sign of weakness. Many of us see brokenness as a sign of failure, that result in fear, disappointment, struggles and we become overwhelmed. Brokenness exist in the places of our lives where we struggle and are afraid to fail. Brokenness for many of us is a source of shame, and resentment. However, is there more to brokenness than this narrow worldview in which we examine the cracks of our lives? Brokenness, for me, is not about weakness; it is about strength. It is about the ability to look at our journeys and see the places where need to grow and develop. Brokenness is learning to be ok with being an unfinished person.

We sometimes forget that God is growing us, and developing us throughout this journey. It is through our struggles that we begin to recognize the presence of God, and our abilities with the help of God to overcome. God will provide us with the very things we need to face every obstacle in this journey we called life. This is not to say that we do not recognize God in the midst of our celebrations and good times. However, it is when we realize that we cannot do it on our own that we tend to call out for God's help. It is in our brokenness that we rely on the power, and the presence of God to show up in our situation.

In 2Corinthians 12:9, Paul, the apostle of Jesus Christ, is a great example of weakness leading to strength in God. Paul writes about asking Jesus three times to remove an affliction in his life. Jesus reminds him that His grace alone is enough. We are sometimes guilty of complaining, feeling shame, and embarrassment about our struggles in this Christian journey as result of how we view the struggles. The truth is we are not recognizing what God is doing in our lives through those situations. We have been taught that our weakness is a sign of shame, when it's really a time of growing and developing. It is a time where and when God is getting our attention, and bringing us into a new level of life and relationship with Him. It is a result of these situations that we grow, learn, and develop. It is in the crises that we begin to call on Him, and seek His presence. It is in the brokenness of our lives, the dark places, the embarrassing circumstances, the misunderstandings, the failures, the do overs that we recognize our inability to move forward in this journey without God. It is not that any of us have cornered the market on the mishaps of life, but it is what we do when we find ourselves wandering in the desert of brokenness?

We often forget the pain of progress and become complacent. However, a lived life forces us to change, and move. We like having things in life to work out, and live stress free. We want the easy road, absent of struggles. We believe that we are entitled to a certain way of life because we believe in Jesus. We want things to happen, and we do not recognize or value the experience. For some of us the experience may seem extreme, but in reality, it is just what we needed to get us to where God destined us to be. It is not that God sends midnight journeys into our lives just to cause us pain. We must ask ourselves: *As a result of this experience what did I learn? As result of this situation, how has my life improved? As result of going through what I been through, how can I help someone else?*

When we only focus on the pain, we do not see the potential in what is before us. Our journey is not just about who we are, but who God is, and what we are becoming. We must realize we are not finished products. We are still growing and developing. If our feet were still growing, and the shoes we love no longer fit. We will either suffer wearing too small shoes, or we will branch out and get some new shoes. I know that metaphor may seem simple, but we must see life progressively, and not passively. In this journey there are things and time that will no longer fit, and we are forced to make a change. This is a journey. I am learning to be ok with the fact that I am broken, and God is at work in my brokenness.

Brokenness is having the ability to know that I am not finished, and I am still a work in progress. Brokenness is learning to become ok with knowing that I am not going get everything right the first time. Brokenness is learning to gain knowledge, and wisdom from our life's experiences. Too often we look at the dark side of our lives, and do not realize it is because of what we went through that we seek to be and do something different. Life will not always be pleasant, and things will not always workout the way we planned or thought, but that does not mean it is not worth it. In this life we will experience turbulence, and the road will get bumpy, but if we push through the rough experiences we will get closer to our destination. Too often we are guilty of quitting to soon, and leaving before the opportunity happens.

Our lives are filled with challenges and opportunities, the question of "what will we do with these life situations" is before us. It is critical that we do some self-reflection, and recognize that we are not perfect and we are ok. It is ok that we could not handle the storm all by ourselves. It is ok that we needed help. It is ok to know that we do not have all together. It is ok to be broken, and know that we are broken. We have been taught and conditioned to be ashamed of our brokenness, but we must learn in being broken we grow and develop. I AM BROKEN and I AM OK!

Our challenge is to learn contentment. Contentment is learning to be satisfied regardless to the circumstances in our lives. When we are not satisfied, we tend to chase what we think will bring us satisfaction without a recognize where we are. The challenge for us is learning what will give us real contentment? For many of us we will never achieve contentment because we never define it for our lives. We do not know what we are really seeking, and why we are seeking it. When we do not know what satisfy us, we will live with no sense of direction or destination. We will live without purpose and fulfillment.

The apostle Paul reminds us in the scripture that his life was one of chaos, chasing what he perceived was the fulfillment in life, and the will of God for him. However, Paul had a Damascus Road experience (Acts 9: 1-6), Paul's life was filled with challenges and he was oppressed by the people he sought to serve (2 Corinthians 11:25-33), moreover he learned to be content in whatever state of life that he was in.

> **Philippians 4:11-13 New Century Version (NCV)**
> I am not telling you this because I need anything. I
> have learned to be satisfied with the things I have
> and with everything that happens. I know how to
> live when I am poor, and I know how to live when I
> have plenty. I have learned the secret of being
> happy at any time in everything that happens,
> when I have enough to eat and when I go hungry,
> when I have more than I need and when I do not
> have enough. I can do all things through Christ,
> because he gives me strength.

My life was overwhelmed with a need for more, but I did not know what the more was. It was like a person who experiences phantom pain after a limb has been removed. Phantom pain is defined as a painful sensation that comes from the limb that has been removed and is no longer there. The limb is gone, but the pain is real. The pains continue until the brain registers that the limb is no longer there. In my ministry I have pastored two persons who had limbs removed. When I visited with them, they were experiencing pain and discomfort. During my visit I witnessed their pain, and called for the nurse to get relief for their struggle, only to be informed that it was phantom pain. I realize that we will never achieve a sense of contentment because we experience phantom dissatisfaction. It has not registered in our mind, body, or spirit that we have gained what we need to move forward in life. So, we continue to seek what we already have.

My wife asked me once, "when is enough, enough?" She really was asking me to define that illusive place in life when I would be content? When we do not know what contentment looks like; what it feels like; what it tastes like; what it smells like; we'll never know what we are seeking. As a result, we will never know when we have it.

While living out of control we do not recognize where we are. We are seeking things that we have already achieved, and gained. We are so into getting, we forgot how to appreciate what we have gained. We are in a hurry for next, that we missed being present in our right now. We cannot focus on where we are because we are too busy trying to get where we are going. My struggle focused on what I was becoming, because I did not know how to become, and how to arrive at becoming. I did not know how to be satisfied or how to appreciate what was before me. I was chasing and pushing at the same time sabotaging the life that I was achieving. I did not know how live in contentment.

I know now that I was living a reckless life. I was seeking things that did not satisfy, because I did understand what satisfaction is all about. Self-reflection helps us to gain a perspective in this life journey of becoming. It is challenge of recognizing that we are broken, and being ok.

We must spend time with ourselves learning who we are, and become aware of what we are becoming. Too often we are chasing what we cannot define. We are in the midst of chaos, only to find out that it is self-imposed chaos of our own doing and creation. We need to seek to remove imposed limits, and expectations that are not healthy or beneficial for the journey we are destined to achieve. We must come to grips with who we are, and allow the journey to unfold.

I know there are people who believe we must make things happen. I believe that if it is to be in your journey, it will happen. No, it is not to say we must not work at it, or initiate the process, but it is critical to recognize what is destined to be, will be. I strongly believe that God has a plan for all our lives, the challenge for us is getting to know that plan. When we are unaware of God's move in our lives, we tend to work outside of God's desire for us.

Jeremiah 29:11-13 New Century Version (NCV)
I say this because I know what I am planning for you," says the Lord. "I have good plans for you, not plans to hurt you. I will give you hope and a good future. Then you will call my name. You will come to me and pray to me, and I will listen to you. You will search for me. And when you search for me with all your heart, you will find me!

Personal Reflection Questions

1. Why do you do what you do?

2. What gives you joy?

3. How do you define fulfillment as relates to your life?

4. How do you understand success?

5. What does peace feel like in your life?

6. Do you find it difficult to be happy?

7. Do you enjoy being you?

8. How do you define contentment?

9. What does contentment look like as it concerns who you are, and who you are becoming?

10. How will you know when you have arrived?

11. What does arrival in your life look like?

To get the meat out of a walnut

you have to break the shell.

Donna M. Cox

Chapter 2
Joseph's Recognition

Genesis 50:20 New Century Version (NCV)
You meant to hurt me, but God turned your evil
into good to save the lives of many people, which
is being done.

The Biblical account of Joseph's life is not captured in the scriptures by accident. Often, we ignore the fact that God is positioning us to accomplish the greatest good for the kingdom and the household of faith. We cannot see what is happening because we are in the midst of the becoming. We are people who operate and live in the physical realms of life. We must see where we think we want to be. However, do we really understand what it will take to get there?

Life is a journey of good days and bad days. Life is filled with ups and downs. We tend to be attracted to a life that is filled with pleasure, and creature comfort. We tend to ignore that life is a whole package, it is composed of positives and negatives and not only what we like. Life can be challenging, there are times when there will be without, and there are times when there will be abundance. Life has days when it is easy, and days when life is a struggle. Life is not just what we like, but also what we do not like. The moments of frustrations are just as important as the moments of celebration.

I have a friend who reminds me that, "We should not complain about our circumstances when we signed up for it." We seek out the person we desire to marry, but then we complain about their behaviors. We apply for the position, then we complain about the work. We buy the house, then we complain about the bills. We buy the car, then we complain about the repairs. We have children, then we complain about raising them. It is a package deal. It is all or nothing. Too many of us want a Burger-King-slogan life, "Have it your way." We like the finished product, but we do not consider what it takes to get there. We forget that there is a beginning, a middle, and an end. One cannot exist without the other.

Our life's experiences are helping us to become what we are becoming. They are not always the most pleasant opportunities, but nonetheless it is what we need for the time. Out of our brokenness we gain knowledge on what we need to do, who we are, and how we get there. We cannot afford to discount life lessons, for they will have an impact on our journey.

Joseph had a life of ups and downs. Joseph had brothers that were jealous of him (Genesis 37:11), because he was favored by his father. Joseph's father favored him because he had him when he was old (Genesis 37:3). Joseph father's love for him caused his brothers to dislike him. Jealousy so often is not because of who you are, it's because the favor of God, or the blessing of God that is upon your life. People want what you have, they desire to be who you are, and that cause tension in your life journey. This is known as jealousy. However, that also allows for us to grow, and become a better person. Joseph found that within his family environment that people who were supposed to give him support and encouragement were a cause of discomfort and frustration. It was not by happenstance that Joseph's brother treated him the way they did. Joseph's life circumstances helped him become who God had destined him to be. It is because pressure in our lives we move.

Opportunities given to us may cause adverse reactions from others. Everyone will not celebrate with us. However, God chooses who God will bless. Joseph is a good biblical example of being rewarded with the favor of his father. Joseph did not do anything, he was born. His father decided to bless him. Many of us have experienced or been granted kindness just because. It was not that we were any different from others. It was just because the person granting the kindness selected us.

There is a saying in the church world that we use frequently, "favor is not fair." Joseph found himself in a struggle because of the favor his father, Jacob. There are times in this life when we will experience favor, but it comes at a great cost. Everyone is not excited that you are being blessed. Jealousy has a way of showing up, and in people that you would never suspect. However, we cannot afford to lose sight of the fact that God is positioning our lives to achieve what He has destined for us. When we become so preoccupied with the distractions, we forget our destiny. Our destiny is not in the distraction, but it is before us. We must be determined and committed to moving forward, and not making a life of our detours.

Joseph had a dream that he shared with his brothers and his father that caused him great struggles in the family (Genesis 37: 5-11). God spoke to Joseph through dreams. We too have dreams. I believe God gives us dreams, because in our sleep, He can get our full attention. We also must realize that everyone will not be excited about our dreams. Just because we think it is great and that it will be an opportunity for greatness, does not mean that others will see it the same way. For Joseph it was a wonderful dream, but for his brothers it was insulting. Joseph seen his brothers bowing down to him. Joseph seen this as great, but his brothers could not see bowing down to their younger brother as something wonderful.

When we are blessed with the favor of God it does not mean others will be excited. Our dreams can cause stress in our relationships. Joseph's life story is a clear example of people not celebrating a God-given dream. His brothers could not see why he would have such favor and not them. They were older, they had lived longer, they had worked harder, but Joseph got favor. The dreamer may be excited, but the hearers want to know why you, and not them. Just because you see yourself as being blessed, does not mean others will be excited about your blessings. Remember favor is not fair, but it is real.

The blessings of Joseph's life caused him the greatest discomfort of life. Joseph's father blessed him, and his brother were not happy with him because of what his father decided to do. Now God gave Joseph dreams that he shared with his brothers and complicated their relationship even more. Blessings may cause discomfort, but discomfort is not always bad. It is when we are not comfortable that we seek to make a change. God has a way of making situations uncomfortable in order to help us to move toward where He is taking us. It was not that Joseph had a problem with his brother; his brothers had a problem with him.

Sometimes we do not realize that a level of stress goes along with success, moving forward, and achieving. When we desire to move to the next level, do we really count the costs? Moving forward means we must leave something behind. How many of us consider that everything we have cannot move forward with us? Learning to release to gain is a great lesson in life. We must learn how to break free from the creature comforts that make us stay, when God calls us to move. Sometimes God has to break us to free us.

Joseph's brothers plotted to kill him, but instead they sold him into slavery, (Genesis 37:18-28). Joseph brothers wanted him gone. He was favored by their father, and were upset when he shared the dream of his brothers bowing down to him. Too often, we live with a belief of entitlement. We think we deserve a promotion because we have been there longer, but someone else gets the promotion. I am the oldest, but our parents gave the business to our younger sibling. I was next in line, but they brought someone from the outside in. Too often we are sitting waiting, but we have never done anything that indicates that we deserve to move from where we are. God operates differently from the ways of the world. Remember, "favor is not fair."

Many of us struggle when others are being blessed, and we are not. It is not to say that God will not bless us, but are we in the position to be blessed? We want certain things in our lives, but if we had these things could we handle them? I have heard people who desire more, but are not doing anything to get more and they speak about living without. Their belief system is all about knowing how to live with lack. They do not seem to want to try the other side. These people have not realized the consequences, and the responsibility of having more. Many people have been totally destroyed because they got into something that they thought they wanted but were not prepared to handle. How many marriages have fallen apart because people we not mature enough to handle the stress of the marriage? How many businesses fail because people do not know what it takes to operate a business? God wants to bless us but He is also preparing us for the life He desires for us to live. We want things now, but we are not always prepared to handle what we want. How many people win the lottery only to find themselves in more debt, and under greater stress?

Joseph's brothers were angry at Joseph, but what did they do to stand out, and show that they were ready for the next level? Many of us want more, but we are not good stewards with what we have. What are you doing now to prepare for the next level? Have you read a new book? Have you surrounded yourself with people who think differently than yourself? Have you attended a seminar, workshop, conference that expose you to new knowledge? How is your prayer and study time with God? We want what we have not been prepared to handle. God has not designed us to fail, but that He may get glory from our lives.

Our journey in becoming can be difficult. We must remember we are going to places, and experiencing things that we have never done or may have seen before. There is a level of frustration in the dealing with the unknown. Our journey is one of faith, and trust. This journey can and will be stressful, but it is not impossible. The brokenness of our journey helps prepare us to appreciate, and gain wisdom for the next phase of our lives.

Joseph was sold to Potiphar by the Ishmaelites (Genesis 39:1-6). Just because it looks and seem bad, does not always mean it is bad. Joseph was sold into slavery, and then sold to Potiphar. The scriptures tell us that God was with Joseph, and he was a successful man. (Genesis 39:2)
Every act to discredit or distract us from what God desires for our lives does not signal the end, or that we will have to live in defeat. Joseph's brothers wanted to do away with him, and God used it to bless him. Just because it may not start out the way we may desire does not mean the journey will not to lead to a blessed life. Our struggles can help us to become better and stronger. We cannot afford to give up because it looks bad. How many times have we witness the losing team comeback in the last minutes of a game and win. Brokenness is not about defeat, it is about using bad situations to gain new knowledge to face what is before us.

How many times in our lives have we refused to go to an event because it did not look like it would be fun or exciting? How many times have we been guilty of giving up because it seemed too hard? Our struggles and disappoints are life lessons, and stepping stones to the next level in life. We see them as defeat, when they are life experiences that are preparing us to live in the future. How many of us know what is next for us? However, our next depends on our right now. We cannot progress not learning. We must consider what is before us, and learn from life what we may need to be blessed in the future.

Potiphar the Egyptian trusted this Hebrew with everything he owned (Genesis 39:4). Just because we cannot see what God is doing is not a reason for us lose faith. Our hope is in the one who created all humanity. The one who is in the present, the past, and the future all at the same time. Our God is Omnipresent. We are concrete people. We can only see what is before us, but God can see down the road of our lives. Joseph's brother never intended for Joseph to be blessed, they just wanted him gone. Just because people want you gone, may be the best thing in your life.

We do not realize that our struggles can lead to better opportunities. If you did not get laid off, would you have applied to work somewhere new? If the building did not get condemned, would you have looked for a new place to live? If that person had not left your life, would you have made the moves you made? We must learn to redefine our struggles and see them as teachable opportunities and learning moments. How many times in the midst of the struggle have we asked, "God what are you teaching me in this situation?"

Our disappointments can be the greatest lessons in life. How many of us needed a push to get moving? If we are honest, many of us would never move into new arenas unless we are pushed past our comfort level, and beyond our complacency. As a result of Joseph's being forced out of a good place in life, helped him to move to an even better place in life. Jim Collins in his book "From Good to Great" said that good is the enemy of great.

We must always get ready for next. Next is the scary place of life, it is traveling in the unknown while living in the present.

29

We must take advantage of right now, but gear up for what is coming next. Joseph had it good, but what was coming around the corner was going to be even better. Potiphar's wife tried to seduce Joseph but because he was loyal to Potiphar, he refused her advances. His reward for doing the right thing was a prison sentence (Genesis 39:7-20). How many times have we done the right thing only to be rewarded with punishment. Life is not always fair, just as favor is not fair. However, the ways we deal with our dilemmas in life can either derail or advance what we are trying to achieve in this life.

Even though Joseph was in prison, the Lord showed him kindness (Genesis 39: 21-23). God can take our bad situations and make good come from them. Despite a prison sentence, Joseph found favor with the warden, and was permitted to do what he desired.

How often do we recognize what God is doing in the midst of our lowest points of life? Too often we are guilty of focusing only the situation that we don't recognize the blessings of God even in our distress. It is what we go through that helps us prepare for where we are going.

While in prison Joseph was joined by the cupbearer of the King and the King's baker. Both of the men had dreams, and Joseph interpreted their dreams (Genesis 40). Joseph reminded the men that God is the only one who could give meaning to their dreams. (Genesis 40:8)

As servants of God, we must recognize the difference between our abilities and God working through us to make things happen. We should not take for granted that our skills are a gift from God. God has given us the ability to make a difference in the lives of others, and as well as ourselves. Joseph reminds the king's servants that God can do what no one else can. In our lives we to must be reminded of who our God is, and what God can provide.

Joseph interpreted the dream of the cupbearer of the king. He asked the cupbearer to remember him in prison when he was freed. The cupbearer was freed but he forgot about Joseph (Genesis 40:23). We must realize that just because things do not happen in the time that we desire, it does not mean it won't take place. It took two years before the Cupbearer remembered Joseph. We cannot afford to lose hope because it takes time for things to happen.

Many of us are uncomfortable in waiting. We want everything to happen now. We do not consider that we may not be ready for the very things that we are asking God to provide. Many times, God need to prepare our lives to receive that things we are seeking. In our developing or immature state of life, we will may neglect or waste a great opportunity. When we reflect on our lives, how many opportunities that was granted to us, but we were not ready for them. As result discounting these learning moments in our lives, we miss out on a great opportunity for growth and development. How many times have you heard or thought, "If I had the knowledge I have now, I would have handled those opportunities or situations differently?" We cannot forget that God knows what God is doing, and why God is doing it.

It took two years for the cupbearer to remember what He promised. As result of the King's dream Joseph will receive redemption (Genesis 41). Joseph interprets the dream of the King, and made ruler over Egypt. What we must consider that every experience of Joseph's life was preparing him for what was next. So, it is in our lives. What we experience is preparing us for what is next in our journey. The frustration for us is that we cannot see what is before us, but the reality is that life is yet before us. Too often we find ourselves frustrated in the process, when the process is needed for the expected outcomes. Joseph's life is a display of the what we go through is not by mistake, but it building us, and equipping us for what where we are headed.

How often have we realized the skills, the wisdom, and the abilities we have gained are a result of the situations, and circumstances of the life we are living and have lived? Now we able to do things that we never imagined as we recount our life stories. The places and times that have proven to be training grounds for where we are now, and where we are heading. Life is not stagnant, life is ever moving. We may stand still, but life does not stand still.

Joseph is now in charge of all of Egypt's commerce (Genesis 41:41-49). There is a famine and because of his God-given ability to interpret dreams he has been given the position to help the people of Egypt, and those around Egypt (Genesis 41:56-57). Who would have ever known that a little boy interpreting his boyhood dream would be afford an opportunity to help a nation. Too often we are guilty of discounting our youthful experiences, but there is a purpose for what occurs in our lives. Because of the circumstances in Joseph's life he can now be a blessing to his father, and his brother (Genesis 42-47).

Our struggle is that we live in "Chronos," which means time. This mark what happens in our lives in seconds, minutes, hours, days, weeks, and months. We operate in these fixed time frames that we seek things to go according to plan. We are logical people that if a than b. However, the God we serve is not limited by some fixed parameter that we call time. God operations out of "Kairos," which means God ordained time. God knows when it shall happen, and why it should happen. Just because it logical in our time, does not mean that we are prepared in God's timing. Joseph life was in "Chronos" and "Kairos." He lived in the natural order time, but God was directing his steps in the progression of what He wanted to accomplish.

The sufferings we have now are nothing compared to the great glory that will be shown to us.

Romans 8:18

Reflection Questions

1. When recounting your life story what would you add or what would you take away? Why?

2. Life is filled with ups and downs; you may call them peaks and valleys. What peaks (celebrations, or high points) and what are the valleys (disappointments, or low points)? If these did not exist in your life, what kind of life would have you lived?

3. What were your peak or high points in life? How did these events or situations help to improve your quality of life, or improve the quality of life for others?

4. What were your valley experiences or low points in life? How did these events or situations help to improve your quality of life, or improve the quality of life for others?

5. What experiences in life draw closer to God and Why?

6. What experiences caused you to question God and Why?

7. When reflecting on the total picture of your life how has you yesterdays helped you prepare for today?

Chapter 3
Elijah's Dilemma

1 Kings 19:1-4 New Century Version (NCV)
King Ahab told Jezebel everything Elijah had done
and how Elijah had killed all the prophets with a
sword. So, Jezebel sent a messenger to Elijah,
saying, "May the gods punish me terribly if by this
time tomorrow I don't kill you just as you killed
those prophets." When Elijah heard this, he was
afraid and ran for his life, taking his servant with
him. When they came to Beersheba in Judah,
Elijah left his servant there. Then Elijah walked for
a whole day into the desert. He sat down under a
bush and asked to die. "I have had enough,
Lord," he prayed. "Let me die. I am no better
than my ancestors."

How often do we forget what God has done, and find
ourselves in despair? Just because someone may not agree with
us or our direction in life does not mean it is the end of the world.
We will find opposition in this life regardless to what we have
accomplished. We tend to forget the great accomplishment in
our lives because we listen to voices of opposition. The same God
that equipped us and prepared us did not abandon us in the
midst of our next challenge.

Elijah, one of God's greatest prophets, found himself in
despair because of the threats of Jezebel. In our lives we will
come across Jezebels who seek to distract us or derail us from
the destiny that God has planned for our lives. Just hearing the
words flowing from the mouth of our adversary, is no reason to
allow fear to cancel our faith. We become discouraged as if God
has lost His ability to do what He promised.

We give more power to the threats, and make giants of the opposition. How many times in the past have we faced opposition and survived? How many times have we face opposing views, but continued to pursue our course of life? We faced opposition before and have learn to overcome, so why would now be any different? Have we not overcome adverse circumstance in the past? Have we not faced enemies opposed to our success, and our future? What made Jezebel now any greater than what we faced in the past, it is how we have given her the power over our lives?

In most cases the things we fear, never take place. Michel de Montaigne said: "My life has been filled with terrible misfortune; most of which never happened." Mary Hemingway said, "Worry a little bit every day and in a lifetime, you will lose a couple of years. If something is wrong, fix it if you can. But train yourself not to worry. Worry never fixes anything."

Worry robbed Elijah of the faith that he had demonstrated in the past. He witnessed God destroy the priest of Baal, and now Jezebel's word cause fear to overtake him. It is not that fear is bad, we must respect fear, but we cannot afford to lose our perspective on life as result of fear. Elijah is a demonstration of real life. We cannot afford to run from someone who just angry about the outcome of God's power.

God has demonstrated His power in our lives. Time after time God has demonstrated His ability to act in our lives. Not that I am any better than anyone else, but I realize the grace of God in my life. I spoke earlier of having a mitral valve repair, but I did not share that my younger brother had a mitral valve replacement almost at the same time. My younger brother transitioned from this life. In my opinion, my younger brother was kinder, more pleasant, much nicer, and deserved to live much longer. For whatever reason beyond my limited understanding, he transitioned, and God healed me. I am truly grateful to God, and realize the favor of God. I have seen God demonstrate His power in my life over adversities, yet I find myself discouraged when opposition show up. I know God can heal. I know God loves me. I know that God has the wherewithal to overcome any and everything I face in this life, but I still find myself allowing the seeds of doubt, and fear of discouragement to seep into my mind and heart.

Elijah, a great man of faith, allowed the threats of Jezebel to challenge his position of faith. We will come across Jezebels, but we must remember that Jezebel is not greater than our God. John Lubbock said," A day of worry is more exhausting than a day of work." John's words are a great portrayal of Elijah's saga. We give life to the words of the opposition. As a result of giving life to those word of opposition, we begin to lose focus, and spend time and energy on what might happen, and not what is happening. It is not that we will not face opposition, but we must recognize what to do with the opposition.

We must learn to address what is distracting us from recognize the power of God in our lives. Bad news will come and go, but God remains the same. Elijah allow this threat of Jezebel to become internalized. He allowed it to be real in his mind, and therefore his reacted to it in emotionally. He knew what God had done, but he allows the words of Jezebel to become louder, and greater than his experience with God.

Our struggles with the opposition are that we react instead seeing it for what it is. Jezebel was angry that Elijah and his God had dismantled and destroyed the priest and what they worshipped. When we discredit the forces that oppose our destiny, they will seek to regain power and control. She (Jezebel) was responding to what was at her religious core. If Baal could not protect himself from the God of Elijah, what would make

Elijah think that Jezebel had any more power than her god (Baal)? We tend to give power to those with the loudest voice, instead of recognizing the God of our salvation. I have seen people back down because someone was louder, or bigger. Loud or big does not make it automatically right, or does it give us a reason to fear.

Yes, Jezebel was Queen and had authority. However, the ultimate authority belongs to God. Elijah demonstrated this very act in calling down fire from heaven and dismantling their religious display. Jezebel is no different than any of us, religion is a passionate subject. We take offense with attacks on our traditions, and our way of doing things. Jezebel recognize the defeat of her god, was a defeat of everything she believed, and what she represented. Therefore, her attack on Elijah was one of revenge and a challenge of power. Moreover, for her to kill Elijah would allow for her to reestablished what she had lost.

Jezebels attacks are often about power that belongs to God. They are seeking to maintain control and see you as a threat. God is sovereign and He reigns. We are instruments of faith that God use to establish His reign in the earth. When our focus is on the threat, we forget our sovereign God.

How many times in this life have we given into bad news, and forgotten about who's really in control. We become depressed, we sing the blues, and act fatalistic. We act as if it is all over. For us in those moments it is real. The cloud of despair lingers over our lives, and we cannot seem to break through it. When we focus on the one negative thing, we forget to look at all the positive things that are taking place. The negativity in our lives take control in ways that we never imagined.

We are emotional beings, God created us that way. Emotions are not a bad thing, but we need understand the difference between emotions, and reality. Have our emotions robbed us of our logic? One incident is not a reason to give up on life, and our life's work. We have face disappointment before and we have survived, so what makes this any different? We often forget the life lessons we have gained as result of what we have experienced in this journey. It is not by happenstance that we lived through, or gone through what did. Each situation is a lesson for the next step we will take.

Elijah believed in God. He preached the message of God. He listened to the voice of God. However, when his life was on the line, he stops focusing on God. For some of us it may have been a termination letter, or a cheating spouse, or a divorce notification, or a bad diagnosis, no matter the issue our God has not changed. As we wrestle with our lives, and the dilemmas we face in this life, we must allow our life lessons to aid us in overcoming the next obstacle that confronts our lives.

What do you do in the face of fear? Many times, fear cause us to forget what we have learned, and focus on what is the source of fear. Too often what is before us is a result of what We have faced in the past. The presence of fear is not the problem, it is when we allow fear to takes control. When fear takes control, it directs and set the course for us to travel. Fear makes us act in the way that is not associated with what we have accomplished, or even what we believe. Absence of fear or when fear is under control we follow the teaching, and operate in the manner that we believe is the best. Fear causes us to operate out fight or flight mode, in which we abandon all of our cognitive skills. When fear is under control we process the situation, and rationally come up with the best approach based on the tools we have to operate. It is not that we will not encounter fear, it's what to do when we are facing fear.

When we are gripped by fear we cannot function as we should. We are afraid to make a move. We question our ability, and the ability of the God who sent us. Fear has a way of shorting out our thoughts, and knowledge. Fear become the conductor of our lives. Fear causes us to freak out in situations that we once had full control.

We cannot afford to forget that God knows the end of the story, while we are still trying to get there. If God declares it, we must recognize that He has inside information. God is Omnipresence, He is everywhere at the same time. He is in our past, present, and future all at the same time. He knows our beginning and our ending. God is Omnipotent, He is all powerful. There is nothing that exist that God could cannot handle. Everything on earth, and in heaven is subject to our God. God is Omniscience, He is all knowing. God knows what will, and what should happen.

Reflection Questions?

1. What is the greatest cause of fear in your life?

2. Have you ever been in a situation where you were not in control? Describe it.

3. Fear is giving control over to your thoughts and imagination, and not taking into account the facts. How many times in your life have you been fearful of something, that never took place?

4. What can we learn from fear?

5. Does the Bible say about fear? Fear Not appears about 365 times in the Bible, why do you believe it occurs so many times?

Come Out of Hiding
Donna M. Cox

Chapter 4
The what-ifs of Moses

Exodus 4:1 New Century Version (NCV)
Then Moses answered, "What if the people of
Israel do not believe me or listen to me? What if
they say, 'The Lord did not appear to you'?"

How often have we been paralyzed by the "What-Ifs" of
life? We tend to focus on the negatives before we recognize the
positives. The "what ifs" are a great distraction that derails us
from what we know to be true. Most of the time the "what ifs"
never happen, but we have given them power to keep us from
operating out of the teachings, and life lessons that we know to
be true.

In the face of failure how will we live? Moses was faced
with all his past let downs, setbacks and crises, but despite all of
that God was calling Moses to do a great work. Moses crisis is not
unlike many of ours. How many times have we failed? How many
times have we not accomplished what we set out to do?
However, in spite of all that God recognizes within us the ability
for us to accomplish the task He has destined for us to achieve.
We all have a history, but God knows our future. We often get
stuck in the fear of "what ifs," and become traumatized. The
truth for many of us is that the "what-ifs" never take place.

Moses was born at a time when a decree by Pharaoh went
out to kill all boy babies. (Exodus 1) To born with a target on your
back from birth is a dreadful thought. Moses was not even in the
world and he was targeted for annihilation. However, his mother
placed him into a basket and strategically floated the basket with
him in the place where the Pharaoh's daughter was bathing.

(Exodus 2:1-9) The circumstances of Moses life are a great indication of the power of God over the "What-Ifs" of this life.

What if someone hears the baby?
What if Pharaoh finds out about the baby?
What if Pharaoh's daughter refused the baby?
What is the basket does not hold him?
What if the basket leaks?

We often play many mental games with ourselves to prevent us from living in faith. We start with failure first, and not success. We contemplate the worse situations in life before we recognize the possibility of the good. Too often we forget about what we believe and why we believe what we believe. Faith is not about having all the answers, it is about believing in the one with the answers. Faith does not mean everything will happen just as we pictured it, but faith stands in the face of let downs, setbacks, obstacles, and build on them. Faith pushes us to achieve the very things that we were destined to achieve.

Moses was faced with the challenge of honoring what God had called him to do, or to allow discouragement to take control of his decisions. We are not any different than Moses. How often have we rehearsed why it will not work, and instead of believing in what has been declared? The greatest defeat in our lives is our inability to believe, and act on that belief. It is a result of fear that we refuse to act. Failure is not our enemy, but fear is.

How did we get to this point in our journey?
What were the circumstances that lead us?
to this moment?

We cannot afford to discount or forget our life's stories. The issues and situations, and setbacks were building blocks to enable us to accomplish what is before us. Too often we forget in face of every crisis we found the strength to overcome. It was not by happenstance that Moses was born, or that his mother sought to defy the decree of the Pharaoh. It was not a coincident that Pharaoh's daughter was bathing and the mother released the basket in the Nile where she was. God is allowing our life's journeys to play out, so we can achieve the life that God has designed for us to live. God is working in us His plan that we may achieve the destiny He has designed for our lives. We allow our fears, and the circumstances surrounding us to disqualify, derail us, distract us from that which God has declared for us. God takes broken people and do great things. In the midst of our brokenness we recognize the power and the strength of our God. Brokenness allow for us to recognize our inability, and God's ability to do what He has declared to be done. We know that we did not accomplish this on our own. The prophet Jeremiah makes it known that God has a plan for our lives. It is our challenge to live in that plan. (Jeremiah 29:11)

It was not by mistake that God choose Moses to do what God needed to be accomplished at that time. Moses was looking at his ability and not God's power. How many of us are guilty of looking at our ability, and not what God can do? When we begin to measure our success based on what we can see and do, we miss what God is doing in our lives. Our God has no limits.

When God calls us to do a "God only thing" in our lives, we must trust God to do what He has decreed to come to past. We are vessels or conduits that God uses to accomplish His will in the earth. We must learn to yield to God, and allow Him to work through us. God does some of His greatest work with broken vessels. How many times have read in the Bible of imperfect, and not all together servants of God doing great things for the kingdom.

Moses biggest dilemma was his past, and other people's perception of him. Moses is not unlike many of us. We all have a past. Have you not heard it said, "There is good in the worst of us, and bad in the best of us?" This old adage is a reminder that God uses imperfect people to do His perfect will. No matter who we are, we all have a story. No, my story may not be like your story, but we all have a story. Moses past encounters in Egypt haunted him, and that caused him to question God's choosing of him. Have you not had a moment when you questioned "why me?" Why would God ask me to do this with all my baggage, and my history? When we operate, and live life based on our abilities alone, we forget God is working in us. Life reminds us that there is one greater than us, accomplishing in us the things that are before us.

There are many great things in our lives that have taken place, and it was not us doing it. Maybe it was a promotion that we did not see coming. Maybe it was a career opportunity that we did not meet all of the qualification, but we got the position. Maybe it was when our credit was below average, but we were approved anyway. Whatever you might call it, I believe a higher power intervened, and I know that power to be God. The God who existed before the world began.

Moses wrestling within himself could not deny the God provided and gave him the life he lived in Egypt. Now Moses was faced with his next move, and he allowed fear to blind side him. We must recognize that God has made provision for what we face in this life. God gave Moses what he needed to accomplish the task that was before him. God will equip us with what we need to achieve what He is asking us to do.

Our preoccupation with doubt, fear, and self-imposed anxiety prevents us from recognizing what God has already done. Too many of us are looking for something outside of the life God has given us to live. The tools Moses needed for the job, God provided. What have God provided for us tools to accomplish the task and maybe we have been ignoring? Was it that opportunity to go back to school, but we say we do not have time? Was it the opportunity to start a business, but we say we do not have the capitol? Was it that new venture in a different state or a different city, but we fear it is too far from family and friends? Was it that new career move, but we say it not the right time in our lives? One thing is for sure, there is never a right time. We can always find an excuse why not to do something. Our challenge is to find the reason why we should risk it all and go for it. Is there a better time than now? We have delayed our destiny because we allow fear of "what ifs" to block the "what is." The what ifs have kept us at the starting gate, when we should be in the race.

We must realize in this life, everyone will not be in favor of what God has called us to do. Some people will come up with better excuses than us, why we should not do what we need to do. Ask yourself, "Are you passionate about it?" "Did you prepare for this moment in your life?" "Will you regret not attempting?" "Are you afraid?" You are normal and there is nothing wrong, we just need to have faith and go for it. Failure is not the problem, fear is. Even if we do not succeed, we learn from the experience, and we know what to do the next time.

My first move from my hometown was in the middle of the night; in a moving truck; with a new wife (a helpmate Genesis 2:18); to a place I had never been to in my life. Little to no money and scared to death, but I believed that this what God desired for my life. Off to seminary, in a city where I knew no one, but I had faith. I knew God had prepared me for this moment in my life. I watch God provide for tuition, housing, and an incredible life journey. God was calling me to a place where I would trust Him to lead me and guide me. A place where I was not relying on my skills, what I had and who surrounded me.

Moses had to trust God, and what God was doing with his life, and so must all of us in this journey. No, it will not always make sense, but if did we would need faith. My life's motto is to from the theme of Star Trek - "To boldly go where no man has gone before." We cannot accomplish this controlled by the "what ifs" of this life.

Moses was frightened because of his skill set. Moses was faced with the biggest job of his life, and just did not fill qualified. So often we want God to provide for us the greatest opportunities known to humanity, but we have never prepared for what we asked God to provide. It is not that God cannot provide, but what are we going to do when we get there? Too many are not taking advantage of our time and opportunities to prepare. We now live in a time when we want to be called, and not prepared. If Moses needed preparation time, what about us?

Are we asking God for something that we have not prepared ourselves to accomplish? What do we bring to the table? What knowledge and tools are we gaining to do what we are asking from God? In this journey we must ask ourselves, "What are we doing to prepare for what we are asking for?" It is easy to ask, but it is just as easy to prepare.

Yes, Moses was prepared and he did not know it. No, Moses did not take a class on "Pharaoh negations", but he was raised in the Pharaoh's palace. Moses was trained by the same person who trained the Pharaoh to be a ruler. Moses learned and gained the skills needed to lead the people and run Egypt one day. No, Moses did not know that he was being trained to lead the people of God out of Egypt, but he was gaining the knowledge needed. How many of us are not taking advantage of trainings opportunities to gain the knowledge to move the next level in our lives?

We live in a time where there is information overload. Life is changing around every second of the day. We want to advance in this life, but we refuse to put the time in to gain the knowledge.

Hosea 4:6 New Century Version (NCV)
My people will be destroyed, because
they have no knowledge. You have
refused to learn, so, I will refuse to let
you be priests to me. You have forgotten
the teachings of your God, so, I will
forget your children.

Our lack knowledge prevents us from being effective, and capable of the task before us. Desire alone is not enough to do a good job. Calling and preparation are important. God provides opportunities for us to gain knowledge but there are times when we ignore the opportunities that are before us. Many churches, local libraries, colleges, seminaries, banks, and civic organization offer trainings, workshops, and seminars for little to no cost and we do not take advantage. YouTube is a wonderful source to hear experts in many different fields share knowledge, and enighten us. Webinars and online classes are gaining more popularity every day. The availability of knowledge is ever before us; however, we must take advantage of these opportunities. What we learn today may be key to our success tomorrow. Moses' history helped equip him for the task that God had called him to accomplish. What we are learning is not by mistake; it is preparing us for what God has next in our lives. We

49

cannot start and get ready; therefore, we must be ready before the opportunity comes.

While Moses had the "what if" syndrome, God had prepared him for the task. Moses' life experiences and circumstances prepared him to do what God was calling him to accomplish.

Life is filled with many uncertainties. Each day is a new journey, and another road to travel. Many times, we are traveling without a map, but nonetheless it is our road to travel. Just as Moses was faced with a return trip to Egypt, with uncertain of what was before him God equipped him for the journey. As God equipped Moses, so will God equip each of us who are obedient, and will listen to His voice.

Reflection Questions

1. What is certain in life?

2. Most things in life are possibilities and we must learn to live with or deal with whatever may happen. How do you prepare to deal with the uncertainties of this life?

3. What are the effects of worry on your life?

4. When you are preoccupied with the possibilities of "what-if," what do you accomplish?

5. How many times have what-ifs distracted you from what is? How do these distractions prevent you from taking advantage of the moment?

6. How has your past life prepared you for your present and future life?

Our Deepest Fear[1]

Our deepest fear is not that we are inadequate.
Our deepest fear is that we are powerful beyond measure.
It is our light, not our darkness that most frightens us.
We ask ourselves, who am I to be brilliant, gorgeous,
talented, fabulous?
Actually, who are you *not* to be?
You are a child of God.
Your playing small does not serve the world.
There is nothing enlightened about shrinking so that other people
won't feel insecure around you.
We are all meant to shine, as children do.
We were born to make manifest the glory of God that is within us.
It's not just in some of us; it's in everyone.
And as we let our own light shine,
We unconsciously give other people permission to do the same.
As we are liberated from our own fear,
our presence automatically liberates others.

---

[1] Marianne Williamson, A Return To Love: Reflections on the Principles of A Course in Miracles

52

Chapter 5
The impatience of Abraham

Genesis 15:3 New Century Version (NCV)
Abram said, "Look, you have given me no son,
so, a slave born in my house will inherit
everything have."

Abram was given a promise by God to make him the father of many nations. Abram struggle with no a promise but not being able to see the possibility of that promise taking place. God promised Abram that he and his wife Sari will have son. For Abram and his wife that seem unrealistic because of their age. Sari when she heard the promise from the angel, she laughed in disbelief. (Genesis 18:12)

How many times in our lives did we not believe the very thing that God has decreed for our lives? We tend to look at the natural and not accept that God knows what God is doing. The frustration for us is that we cannot phantom how God's going get it done. Sari attempted to fix the promise by giving her maidservant to her husband. This only cause greater stress, and confusion. When we step into a "God only situation" we will mess it up. Just because we cannot figure it out, does not mean God needs our help.

I remember that I wanted so bad to leave the city we were staying, that I totally ignored the church and its leadership was making provisions for me to continue my work there. I wanted out, so I could not focus on what God was doing. I was going to make it happen, not paying attention and trusting God. Did I mess things up, yes! My actions, and my refusal to pay attention to what God was doing caused me to hurt the people who were only trying to help me. I ended staying 9 years longer than I ever wanted. Not recognizing that God was fulfilling his promise in my life. I live a self-created exile. Just because we cannot see what God is doing, does not mean we need to help God get it done. That is not say, we procrastinate, but we must be open and willing to do and believe God for His provisions. We must move in the direction and seek the things that allow for us to achieve that which we are seeking. How often have we been engaged in a process and it seemed as though we were not accomplishing anything? Abram knew the promise, but it was not happening as he phantom. When we starting doubting God, it causes an imbalance in our lives. Faith and Fate is not the same. We must learn to operate out of faith, and not become fixated that our present situation is our fate. Abram left all that he knew, and those who he knew, to follow a God who he did not know.

Abram did not have a history with this God, but he had a promise from this God. He trusted this God that was a mystery to him, but something about this God caused Abram to trust in Him. How many times have we struggled in our belief, but we could not stop believing? We have invested too much of ourselves, and we have gone too far to turn around. Faith and Fate or not the same. God will honor His word despite what it looks like.

Matthew 19:29 New Century Version (NCV)
And all those who have left houses, brothers,
sisters, father, mother, children, or farms to
follow me will get much more than they left,
and they will have life forever.

This scripture reminds us that no one has given up anything that God will not bless them with even more. God want us to trust Him despite what it looks like. What we see in the natural does not mean that is how God is operating in our lives.

We must recognize the fact that our vision is limited, but God has no limits.

Abram knew in order for this promise to take place, something supernatural had to take place. Supernatural happenings do not take place because of us, but from a source outside of us. Abram believed despite what it looked like. In this journey we will be faced with believing when nothing within us, or around us suggest anything will happen. How many times have we wanted to know how will it take place? How often have we questioned the process, because it was not logical? We wrestle with the unknown, but God operates in the unknown. What we know takes no faith, but what do know takes faith. When know what we know, we begin to become complacent, what God desires from us is to trust Him.

Many times, we are in a hurry. We live a fast pace world. Fast foods, instant coffee, high speed internet, turbo engines, all indications that we want it now. Waiting for many of us causes unrest within our spirits, and makes us restless. How often have we been guilty of blowing our horn because the driver in front was taking too long to move? How many times have we change lanes in the grocery store because the cashier was not moving fast enough? We are in a hurry, and most times we do not have anywhere to be. Abram was getting older, but God was committed to what He promised. (Isaiah 55:11)

We are excited about hearing and knowing the promises of God, but we struggle with waiting on God to fulfill the promises. Our challenge is not unlike Abram and Sari, it does not always make sense to us. If we cannot understand it, we struggle with believing it. We live in a world of facts, and not a world of faith. God want us to trust Him, therefore we do not have all the answers, but He does. We are limited just because we were created by God, and we did not create God. He (God) is in control of what is next, yet we have free will. No, God will not impose himself on us. God wants us to desire to be in relationship with him, and to trust Him. Too often our godly relationship reflects our natural relationships. We do not trust each other and we transfer those same feeling to God.

Abram and Sari knew their limitations. They were well past the childbearing age. Sari could not see how this would be possible at her age to bear a child. Our limited perspective reminds us that we need something greater than ourselves to accomplished things that are beyond our capability. It is not that it cannot be done, we just cannot do it or do it alone.

Our inability to do it alone is not a bad thing. It is when we do not recognize our inability and try to fix it, or blame others for it. God wants us to trust Him, by bringing before Him what we cannot do on our own. He wants a relationship with his children must move in the direction and seek the things that allow for us to achieve that which we are seeking. How often have we been engaged in a process and it seemed as though we were not accomplishing anything? Abram knew the promise, but it was not happening as he phantom. When we starting doubting God, it causes an imbalance in our lives. Faith and Fate is not the same. We must learn to operate out of faith, and not become fixated that our present situation is our fate. Abram left all that he knew, and those who he knew, to follow a God who he did not know.

Abram did not have a history with this God, but he had a promise from this God. He trusted this God that was a mystery to him, but something about this God caused Abram to trust in Him. How many times have we struggled in our belief, but we could not stop believing? We have invested too much of ourselves, and we have gone too far to turn around. Faith and Fate or not the same. God will honor His word despite what it looks like.

Matthew 19:29 New Century Version (NCV)
And all those who have left houses, brothers,
sisters, father, mother, children, or farms to
follow me will get much more than they left,
and they will have life forever.

This scripture reminds us that no one has given up anything that God will not bless them with even more. God want us to trust Him despite what it looks like. What we see in the natural does not mean that is how God is operating in our lives. We must recognize the fact that our vision is limited, but God has no limits.

Abram knew in order for this promise to take place, something supernatural had to take place. Supernatural happenings do not take place because of us, but from a source outside of us. Abram believed despite what it looked like. In this journey we will be faced with believing when nothing within us, or around us suggest anything will happen. How many times have we wanted to know how will it take place? How often have we questioned the process, because it was not logical? We (creation.) Too often we desire a solo act when it call for a duet or a trio. Life is not always designed to be lived alone. God created a helpmate for Adam, so man would not be alone.

God want us to trust Him and allow Him to lead in this relationship. Sari forgot that this was a God promise. In a God promise that means that God will fulfill what He declared. We are incapable of being God, and doing only God can do. How many times in our own lives have we sought to fix or make happen something that was out of our realm? When we operate in arenas that are not created for us, we tend to make a mess, get hurt, and hurt others in the process. God did not create us to live without Him, but to live in relationship with Him. Abrams promise was from God, due to the relationship he had with God. God showed through His promise to Abram despite human impossibilities the divine has the power to overcome what is impossible for humans.

Too often we want to be independent, when we are called to be in relationship. We desire for things to happen now, but God desire for us to build relationships, trust one another, and grow through the process. The promise should have increased Abram's and Sari's faith, but their impatience caused increased doubt. Many of us will never be good fishermen or hunters because we are too impatient and do not know how to wait. It is not that there are no fish in the lake; it is that we are not willing to let the fish take the bait. it not there are no deer in the forest, it that we are not willing to wait until the deer cross our path. It is not that God is not fulfilling His promise, we are to in a hurry to wait on God.

Waiting is a time of preparation. It should not be a time of frustration, but a time of growth and development. Diamonds start off as coal under pressure for a long period. However, there is a difference in value between diamonds and coal. Pearls start off sand, an irritation to a clam, but over time that irritation become a valuable. There is a difference between the value of sand and pearls. How has our impatience cost us? When we learn to wait and be faithful to the process the results are valuable to our lives.

Reflection Questions

1. What has impatience cost you in life?

2. How has being in a hurry profited your relationship with God, family, and otherpeople?

3. How have you tried to help God answer your prayers?

4. What is the difference between waiting and procrastination?

5. Do you trust God to honor His word?

Adinkra Symbol
Gye Nyame: Except God
God, alone, knows all there is to know about
our situations or our futures. We can trust God.
Donna M. Cox

Chapter 6
King Uzziah's overset

2 Chronicles 26:16 (NCV)
But when Uzziah became powerful, his pride led to
his ruin. He was unfaithful to the Lord his God;
he went into the Temple of the Lord to burn
incense on the altar for incense.

Arrogance and pride can lead to our down fall. What will it cost us when we operate outside of that which we are called to do? Too often we take for granted that people should operate within their skill set, and training. We live in a time when too many of us try to drive in multiple lanes at the same time, and wonder why there is so much congestion on the roadway. When we occupy two lanes at the same time, we prevent other drivers from utilizing the lane. So, it is when we operate outside of our call, or giftedness we cause disasters, and block other from using their skills.

I once thought I could repair a leak in our girls' bathroom. That was the greatest do it yourself disaster in the history of our home. I did not turn off the main water valve, or even knew that there was a shut off valve on the faucet. I removed the faucet to have water all over everywhere. Besides that, I did not know where the main water valve was located. After calling a plumber who told me the proper way to stop the water, and where to find the shut off valves. I heard a voice say, "Stay in your lane." It is not that you cannot multitask but make sure you have the skills, and the wherewithal to do the task at hand.

Although King Uzziah was a good king, and did great things for the people of God, he lost his focus and wanted to operate outside of his position. He was a King and not a priest. He wanted to burn incense before God in the temple, a task reserved for the priest, and not the King. (2 Chronicles 26:16) His pride caused him to lose focus and attempt to do the job that was only for priest. (2 Chronicles 26:18)

Our struggle is recognizing that everyone has a purpose can cost us in relationship with God and humanity. When we learn to value others contribution, we can operate in harmony. There is a reason that some we gifted with one thing, and others we gifted with a different thing. (Romans 12:3) It is not that one is less than anyone else, but we need everyone to function in their giftedness that our community can operate fully.

When one person does too many jobs they begin to think things cannot happen without them. This can easy lead to arrogance setting in, which will allow for pride to overtake them. The King was not a priest, even though he may have known how to do it, it was not his job to get it done. Too often in ministry we have one person wearing too many hats, and the ministry suffers as result. When one begins to rely on their own abilities, and operate outside what they had been tasked to do it impact how people see them, and their effectiveness. At the end of the day the good that they may have accomplished is tarnished by their inability to stay in their lane. God will raise up the right people to do what is needed to be accomplished if we trust and allow God to do it. I have learned that you are not, and cannot do everything you may desire to do. King Uzziah was a good King, but his life ended in isolation as result of his pride.

How often in ministry have we been guilty of not allowing others to do their jobs. No, they may not do things the way we would, but they get it done. I been guilty of "Uzziah syndrome" of doing what others are skilled and know how to do. We must learn to respect that God knows what He is doing, and He equipped those He wanted to get the job done. Just because we want to do it, does not mean we need to do it. God has called us to live in community. How community become comprised is when there is a lack of respect for one another.

Community is a place of learning to appreciate differences and share in the work to accomplish the common good for all. God has gifted everyone in the community with a gift for the betterment of that community. We cannot allow our roles to overrule what God has blessed others to accomplish. When we live outside of our roles or skills, we may cause more problems. We must learn that if we just wait on God, He will bless us with the right person for the job.

We miss great opportunities to teach others new skills, and grow together, because we want thing done our way. Knowledge is great, but knowledge shared is greater. We forget that we are not designed to stay on this earth forever. The things we know, and the skills we have are valuable to the community, therefore we need to share them with others. To many graveyards are filled with knowledge that should have been shared with others, but people died with the valuable knowledge. As a result of the next generation is stuck trying to learn and recreate. We miss the fact that we are blessed to be a blessing. What we have is to help not only ourselves but also those in our community. King Uzziah one of the greatest kings, but his inability to allow the priest to do their job cost him. What does it cost us when we prevent others from operating in his giftedness? Some of the worst advice I have heard was from Christians. You have heard this as well: "Never tell people all that you know, so they will always have to come back to you." "If you share your recipe, always leave out an ingredient so it will not be same as yours."

We have allowed the ways of the world to enter our communities of faith, and even our families that we practice the same deception. God blessed us to tell the story and equip the next generation. What good is our story if the next generation do not have all the pieces. We must ask ourselves why did God entrust me with the knowledge I have? Where did I acquire my knowledge? What good is knowledge if I am the only one with it?

King Uzziah wanted to operate outside of his anointing.

(2 Chronicles 26:16-21) The priest was consecrated to burn incense in the sanctuary of God, but King Uzziah's pride got in his way. Many times, we witness people with natural abilities trying to do what God called others to do, and becomes ineffective in their work. Just because one is a gifted school teacher does not make them a gifted Sunday School teacher. Just because one is good in the business world, does not mean that translate inside the church. Faith overcomes deficits, and sometimes business person cannot see God in the equation. Do not get it wrong, their knowledge is critical and important in the life of the church, but faith principle do not always align up with worldly methods.

King Uzziah was afflicted with leprosy for being unfaith, prideful, and operating outside of his anointing. How has pride prevented us from operating in our lane? Do not misunderstand me, I still believe in do it yourself projects. I still watch the "YouTube Videos" to learn how to fix things. However, I recognize when it is outside of my skills and ability to do certain things. I know that I am limited and that God has placed people in my life, and my community to help achieve what He want done.

In a community it is ok to ask for help. In a community it is ok not to have all the answers. In a community it is ok to trust someone else to accomplish the task at hand. However, when our communities do not have the skills to get it done, it is ok to call someone for help.

What is pride and unfaithfulness costing our communities, and families? Are we adding to a lost generation, because we have not involved the present generation in the process of community leadership? Are we guilty of blocking others from growing, and developing because of our pride to be important, and have things done our way? Are we the force behind our communities being broken, because we die with answers they are seeking? How many ingredients have we left out of the recipe that now it no longer works? How many steps have we fail to tell others about, so now that have no direction?

What story have we forgotten to share? What secret have we forgotten to uncover? Do not allow the grave to rob another generation of the knowledge that can help them navigate through this life.

King Uzziah did not respect the delineation between the monarch and the priestly roles, and it caused him to be punished. God has ordained order, and given us roles to operate within. When we disrespect the roles, we disrespect God. It was not the priest who punished the King, it was God. Our communities need every person within it to function well. It is when we stop allowing people to function in their God given roles that we disrupt the harmony of the community.

Reflection Questions

1. What are your God-given gifts?

2. What do you offer your community of faith, family, and community at large?

3. How to you share your knowledge with others in your community, family, and church?

4. Are you mentoring others in your family, church, and community?

5. What knowledge was lost in your family as result of the death of a patriarch or matriarch?

Chapter 7
Jonah's Pain of Preference and Pleasure

Jonah 1:3 New Century Version (NCV)
But Jonah got up to run away from the Lord by
going to Tarshish. He went to the city of Joppa,
where he found a ship that was going to the city
of Tarshish. Jonah paid for the trip and went
aboard, planning to go to Tarshish to run away
from the Lord.

Jonah is a great example of one that refused to hear and heed to voice of God. How many times did we leave and isolate ourselves rather than to be obedient and honor the godly expectations for our lives? Regardless to the who, the what, the when, or the where, Jonah did what he felt necessary to escape God's request. Sure, we can blame and point the finger, but that will never excuse us from not doing what God has commissioned and required us to do.

There have been many times in ministry, in life, in marriage, in rearing a child that I just wanted to quit, run, hide, and abandon the process. It was not working or going the way I desired. That was my greatest challenge. It was not going the way I desired. Jonah did not follow God's command because it was not going the way he desired. What we desired does not mean it is God's will for our lives. Also, what we desire or seek does not mean that we are prepared to handle that which we are seeking.

Our limited perspective is based our pleasure and what pleases us, more than what please God. We live in a world of preference, and that does not always honor the Word of God. Our entire lives have been shaped by our preferences. We sometimes forget what we preferred does not always work out the way we planned.

67

Jonah wanted God to punishment the people of Nineveh. However, God called Jonah to go to Nineveh and preach. Jonah knew if the people would repent, God would forgive them. We have our Jonah moments in our own lives. We desire for certain people to feel the same pain, or punishment that they inflicted in the lives of others, but God's mercy and grace cancel out our desires.

When we look at our lives, must begin to understand God's grace guided us through the land mines of bad choices, bad decisions, and questionable friendships, shady deals, immoral relationships, and so many other paths we have taken in this life. God has shown great compassion to us, yet we like Jonah ask of this compassionate God to hold back his compassion in the lives of others.

When a mass murderer is sentence we want death penalty. When a serial killer or rapist is sentenced for their crimes we seek punishment and not mercy. The unfortunate reality for many us is that we seek mercy for some, but not the same mercy for all. Justice is blind, it should be absent of our biases. What one deserves, all deserve. Jonah desired Nineveh to be punished for the heinous acts they committed. If Nineveh does not deserve God's mercy, do any of us deserve God's mercy?

Our preferences sometimes lead to greater pain, and not the promises of God we desire. When we seek punishment for someone, what seed are we sowing. The seeds we plant will soon grow into plants, that may grow into trees, and continue to reproduce. Is this really what we are seeking, when we say they do not deserve God mercy? Is one sin greater than another? Does one sin deserve punishment, and others should be forgiven? Jonah is just as disobedient in his refusal to follow through what God had asked of him. Does not Jonah deserve the same punishment that he seeks for Nineveh?

Jonah was willing to give up his way of life, the

68

community he shared to ensure that the people of Nineveh would not get the preach Word of God. Despite our selfish moves in life, we must remember, just as God called us, He can use another to accomplish His will. Jonah's refusal will not keep God's will from being accomplished. How guilty are we, that we desire the punishment for others that we refused to offer the power of the Word of God?

The life that God seeks for us is greater than our likes and dislikes. Our struggles only help to equip us to live the life before us. It would have pleased Jonah to see Nineveh destroyed, but is that what God wanted? The same wrath that we call down on others, is the same wrath we deserve. (Matthew 7:2) We need to be aware of desiring the downfall of others. It is easy to look at the sins of others, but that does not excuse our sins. Would we want the same wrath upon us that we desire for others? We seek mercy and grace for our lives, but do we believe that others deserve the same? Who deserved mercy? Who has the right to determine who gets mercy and who does not get mercy?

When God's expectations do not measure up to our preferences or pleasure, we seek other options. We run like Jonah, or we become a victim of the issues of life. We act as if God is not aware of what He is asking, and we want to remind Him why we should not do what He has asked us to do.

We must come to grips with the fact that everything God desires, will not fit neatly into our plans for this life. Just because we did not want to go, does not mean that is not the place we were destined to be. There have been many times in my life where I did not want to go to an event, or an activity only to have the greatest time of my life. What if I would have avoided attending those events, I would have never met the people who were there, or learned from those experiences.

When we our focus is only on vengeance and punishment, we do not realize the impact it has on our own lives. How much of our lives have been comprised desiring the downfall of others? and the wrath of God to come upon their lives. Too often we are signally focused on someone demise that we miss the big picture. As result we miss what God is teaching us, and what they have to offer. Our preoccupation causes us not to accomplish what we need to do, because we are focused on the downfall of others.

In ministry you will find many people who will oppose what you seek to achieve. People will not agree with your goals in ministry; how you live your life; how you raise your family; and how you do business. I have learned that the people who opposes you are not all evil or bad. They are just as passionate as you are, but see things from a different perspective. The bible reminds us that iron sharpens iron. (Proverbs 27:17) As result of the struggles, and pressure, we become better equipped to serve not just the people before us, be even those in the future.

Our desire for punishment against the opposition, is that a reflection of the love of God in our hearts? The mercy of God is a reflection of God giving us second chance. It is not an excuse for disobedience, for all of us are guilty of sin. As reflection of who God is, and being created in His image we must seek to emulate God in the world around us. We must model kingdom living, by loving those who oppose us, and saying all kinds of evil against us. No, it not easy. If it was easy, Jonah would have never run to Tarshish.

We all will face our own Ninevehs, and God will call us to offer God's mercy. When we allow our hearts to be harden against other people we are not displaying the love of God in the earth. We become bitter, hateful, and evil. We compromise our witness, and we bring shame to the kingdom of God. It is easy to display love and mercy toward those we like, and have a relationship, but what about the outcast, our enemies and the forgotten.

What about the one who broke in our house, and stole our property? The one who robbed us? The person who undermined us? Do they deserve God's mercy? Mercy is not regulated by what we have done right, it is a result of what we done wrong. How many of us stand guilty needing the mercy of God in our lives?

Seeking to live a Godly life will not always make sense in the world we live. A Godly life will not always fit neatly into our logic models, but God love is greater than our sins. God ask of us to love like He loves, and bless like He blesses. We must learn to see other through the eyes of God, and not through our eyes of pain, shame, humiliation, regret, and getting even. Jonah knew of God great love for humanity, and God's desire for humanity to repent and return to God. However, Jonah ran as if the offer would have been removed from the table.

Has our anger blinded us from seeing what God sees? Have our pain blocked the mercy of God from being revealed? How can we love God, and hate at the same time? We all are guilty before God, however because of Jesus' blood we can stand in the presence of God. No, it does not excuse what we have done, but if God forgives, we must learn to forgive as well. Just because we may prefer wrath, God mercy abound even more.

Hate is not a byproduct of the love of God. We can oppose what people say, and even how they live, but we must learn to love them anyway. Our world has become so bitter that we have forgotten how to love? Now we sit and wait for the destruction of those we hate, and they sit and wait for our destruction. We must learn to look at one another and see the image of God within each of us, and learn to love that image. Jonah refused to see the image as result of his anger.

Are we guilty of wanting Nineveh to be destroyed? What is our Nineveh? Is it the people who look different than we do? Is it the people who live on the other side of the tracks? Is it the people who do not have what we have? What is our Nineveh? Is it the people who made a different choice in life? We may not agree with how people live, but all people are made in the image of God. And God, alone, is responsible for helping them shape that image in the correct way.

Reflection Questions

1. Who deserves God's mercy?

2. Have you committed any sins?

3. What makes one person better than another?

4. Who deserves justice?

5. What does Micah 6:8 mean to you?

6. What does the image of God look like in another person?

7. What does the image of God look like in you?

Made In The Image of God

Chapter 8
When Cockiness leads to confusion

Genesis 11:4 New Century Version (NCV)
Then they said to each other, "Let's build a city
and a tower for ourselves, whose top will reach
high into the sky. We will become famous. Then
we will not be scattered over all the earth."

When we are too busy making everything about us, we forget who has blessed us with what we have. Ministry is one of many professional areas where our egos can get in the way. We want everyone to look at us, instead of the one who is working through us. We sometime misplace our focus on the objects and not the provider of the objects.

Ministers and those in ministry can get with psychologist call the "Savior Complex." It when we start to believing that things happen as result of us. We believe that we are the single reason that people's lives are changing, that projects are completed, and so on. It is the loss of humility and an increase in pride. Sometimes we forget that pride goes before the fall. (Proverb 16:18) We like the light to shine on us, and the attention to be about us, that we get caught in praise that belongs to God. (Ephesians 3:20,21)

The Tower of Babel story is a great story that indicates the power of working together, but also shows what happens when we lose focus. It is so easy to lose focus in ministry whether it is a success or a failure. We can get impressed with ourselves, and our ability that we lose our humility. This affects how we honor and worship God, and how we relate to others.

When our language is about what we have done, we forget what got us to that point of achievement. We forget all those who sacrificed, and gave of themselves so that we can enjoy the very thing that we are claiming to have accomplished. The old adage is true, no person is island, and no person stands alone. There is a reason for us to live in community, because we are better together than we are alone. One struggle we have in this American competitive culture is learning to share and be transparent in our work, and ministry. We want greater, better, and more, and have lost the need to be content and grateful. (Philippians 4:11)

Our focus is purely on our ability, we must ask ourselves what happens when we can no longer do what we do now? Life is progressive and what we can do now, we may not be physically or mentally capable to accomplish later in life. This should help us put life into perspective, that we will not be here always. The graveyard is filled with talents and skills that people never passed onto a new generation. How many recipes and methodology fill the graveyards because of our selfishness, and pride would not allow for us to share and teach others. We cannot afford to make everything about us, and advance the cause of Christ in this world.

In Genesis 11:4 the people were concerned with becoming famous. How many times have we heard people wanting their names celebrated that they refuse to share what they had to offer. The sad reality is that people will stay in a position in church until they die, instead of training younger people to work in that position. We have forgotten that everyone can be replaced. We have forgotten that God does not have a shortage on skills, talents and gifts. We cannot afford to allow our egos to get in the way of the glory of God.

How often have we allowed our talents and skills to control our focus? No man has accomplished anything on their own. We are the benefactors of the labor of those who have gone before us. We benefited from their errors, as well as their success. Many of us have lost our focus because we have made everything about us in order to make a name for ourselves. When it becomes about us, it does not become about the God who has equipped, empowered, and enlighten us to accomplish what we have in this life. We become a god to ourselves. We believe that we did it on our own, our pride swells, and we become arrogant.

The bible reminds us that pride goes before the fall. (Proverbs 16:18)

I had experienced ministry success in my early years as an assistant to a pastor. Those years we exciting, and frightening all at the same time. Boy to hear people share how wonderful of a job I was doing was great, but each ministry opportunity brings with new challenges. I must admit, I was not afraid of the challenges, but I was never prepared for the failures to come so close together. Learning how to deal my ministry failure was more than a notion. I never considered the human factor. You know the personalities of those you serve. The power of the walk way (those who leave the ministry), and the secret culture of traditions. I forgotten that everyone did not want to change, and those who opposed change will oppose the person who is proposing change. I was not prepared for the fights. I was accustomed to the supportive community that wanted what was next. I got caught up into a ministry of success that was based on one community, and not the one I was facing. We can never take for granted that what worked in one place will work in another. God had not changed, but I was relying on my skills, and abilities, and not my faith, and His word. God had to confused the language that I would come to grip with recognizing Him, and not myself.

I misjudged that the adversary is an accuser of the believer. (Revelation 12:10) The impact of the attacks was not the ministry life with which I was acquainted, so I was not prepared to handle it. Sometimes, success can blind you to what is next.

Our desire to become the next rising star, the next great name, the next golden child can tarnish the person we are in God, and the relationship we have with God. To many of us are paying the price for losing our humility, and not allowing God to move us in His time.

We want it now, and we want it in a hurry, but we are not always prepared to handle what we want. Losing our way is more common than we realize. Napoleon Hill asks the question in his work on *Think and Grow Rich*, "What are you willing to give up to get what you want?" Sometimes God has to reminds us by taking us backwards in order to bring us forward. God' knows the plans He has for our lives, we must seek to hear His voice, and live out those plans. We become frustrated when our plans clash with God's plans, and we miss the mark.

Have we taken into account what it will cost for fame and fortune? We do not hear the behind scene stories and we only see the finished products. We see the glitz and the glamour but we did not understand the investment, and the sacrifice. Many do not know of the restless nights, the early morning meetings, and the late-night phone calls. Many are not aware of the secret letters with no return address. Napoleon Hill is right when he asks, "What are you will give up to get what you want?" God stepped in as they built this tower that we know as the Tower of Babel, because the people lost sight of Him. The tower was about their fame and glory. Sometimes in ministry we caught up building a great ministry for our own ego. We looking to have great achievements, not for God's glory, but for our fame. God has to reminds us that He will guide us, but we cannot lose sight of Him.

The challenge that all of us face is not losing focus. Another challenge is realizing that God has not forgotten us in our success as well as our failures. God is faithful and we must learn to trust Him. We may be skillful, and have the abilities to be great and do awesome things, but it is by God grace. I am often reminded that some of the smartest people, and most brilliant minds never spent one day in the limelight. May of the smartest people on earth name will never be called, or will ever be listed in a book, but nonetheless these great people have so much to offer. It is when we lose focus, and are caught in fame that we forget our mission and purpose.

Reflection Questions

1. Name everything that you are an expert?

2. How did you become so efficient, and skillful in these areas?

3. Were you born knowing what you know?

4. How much of what you know did you learn from another source?

5. We are a product of others' investments. Whether dead or alive, many people gave themselves to provide us with the knowledge that we now master. We have not achieved whatever it may be isolated. Our perceived greatest is a result of someone's sacrifice. Who do you need to thank for the success in your life?

Chapter 9
Fighting against the wrong enemy

Acts 9:4 New Century Version (NCV)
Saul fell to the ground and heard a voice saying to him, "Saul, Saul! Why are you persecuting me?"

I believe that the adversary knows the power of unity that he seeks to cause discord or confusion to prevent us from achieving our goals. Saul, you know him as Paul, was passionate about God and his relationship to God. However, Saul was caught up and destroying that the very thing God was establishing. Saul sought to destroy everything that challenged his way of worshipping God and serving God. Saul's battles sound like the same worship wars, and church battles that exist within today's church.

Not only do we find battles within the church, but within our personal lives, families, and in ministry. We tend to attack what we do not understand, and anything that challenges us in faith. These challenges come from those within and outside of our ministry or personal circles. As a result of battling within the church and religious circles, we spend time battling the people instead of doing ministry. How distract have we been with internal battles, that it prevented us from moving the ministry and the church forward? Saul was guilty of a common reaction from people whose way of doing thing is challenged. When our way of doing things is challenge, we seek to silence the opposing forces. The sad truth is that the people who sought to follow Jesus and his way were the people Saul sought to persecute. How many times have we been guilty not taking the time to learn and understand what is happening before we made judgements? Just because it is not our way or preference of worship does not make it wrong.

How many times have we heard of church battles? How often have we heard of infidelity among the clergy? How often have we heard of the moral failure of church leaders? These situations have a way of turning people, even ourselves against the church and the ministry. As long as we focus attention on our differences and shortcomings, we take our attention away from the work of the church and the ministry. We also put the church and the ministry in a position to be criticized by those who needed it most. Too often the members of the faith community are the greatest critics of the church. We must learn how to build the church and not be guilty of destroying the church.

Where do hear about the struggles of the church? Where do we hear about the moral failure of members of the church? Who criticizes the church the most? It is unfortunate that many of the people who attend the church are as guilty as Saul was on the Damascus Road.

As humans we all have sin issues. However, as result of birth, death and resurrection of Jesus Christ we were made right with God. Through blood of Jesus and accepting the salvation Jesus offers, we have been redeemed. All of have committed an act that is not pleasing to God at some point in our lives. Yet we sought the compassion of God to forgive and redeem us from our sins. Just as we seek to forgiven and restore, we must seek the same for others. It is not that we excuse sin, but we do condemn those around for committing the same offenses.

Saul in his passion to put down an uprising of Jesus followers was attacking the church that God was establishing. Saul viewed the sons and daughters of God as his enemy, because they went to a different church. Saul was concerned with heresies that attack the Jewish way of worship that he missed the mark. How often are we guilty of the same persecution of the church and of those who do things different than we are would like?

Church wars may not end until Jesus returns, but we need to recognize that the more we fight each other, the less time we have to battle against the real enemy (satan). The enemy continues to cause havoc in this present generation. The enemy that calls into question our sense of morality and ethics. The enemy is destroying families, and killing innocent lives. The enemy of hatred, and bigotry. The enemy of racism, classism, and elitism. The enemy that leads to poverty, homelessness, and extend prison sentences.

While we are fighting each other, the adversary is stealing the minds and the hearts of another generation. While we are battling over non-significant matters, the souls of our children are being lost. Too often we are missing the fact that at the end of our religious wars there are no winners, but only losers. When we spend our energy battling one another in the church, who is bringing forth the message of hope to the world?

Saul is a great example of person who was broken and didn't know it until he encountered Jesus on the road to Damascus.

In your brokenness have you had an encounter with Jesus? Are you *ready* to encounter Jesus?

Reflection Questions

1. When have you been persecuted each other in the church?

2. Have you ever witnessed a church fight?

3. What was the result of the fight?

4. Have you ever experienced church hurt?

5. As result of church hurt how do you feel?

6. Why do believe there is so much division in the church?

7. What should the church really be focusing on?

Because of this decision, we don't evaluate people by what they have or how they look. We looked at the Messiah that way once and got it all wrong, as you know. We certainly don't look at him that way anymore. Now we look inside, and what we see is that anyone united with the Messiah gets a fresh start, is created new. The old life is gone; a new life burgeons! Look at it! All this comes from the God who settled the relationship between us and him, and then called us to settle our relationships with each other. God put the world square with himself through the Messiah, giving the world a fresh start by offering forgiveness of sins. God has given us the task of telling everyone what he is doing. We're Christ's representatives. God uses us to persuade men and women to drop their differences and enter into God's work of making things right between them. We're speaking for Christ himself now: Become friends with God; he's already a friend with you.

2 Corinthians 5:17 MSG

Chapter 10
I am Broken

We live in a world that believes in perfection, and being number one. I agree that all should seek to be the best we can be. So often we lose who we are chasing some abstract image of perfection, instead of seeking to reflect the image of God. The chase to be better than someone else, and to have what other may not have is a hard road to travel. We are challenged to be the best person we can be, and honor the call of God upon our lives.

In this journey we need critical self-reflection which is not always easy, but it is needed. The Bible is filled with many imperfect people who God used to do His perfect will in the earth. There are many more accounts that I could have drawn from for this book. However, the best account is one own story. To recognize that we do not have life all together and learn to be ok with that is counter cultural. It does not fit with the norm. I personally think we spend too much time trying to fit in, when Jesus called us to peculiar people. (I Peter 2:9)

Making every effort to be perfect, and holding people to a level of piety caused me to have unbelievable stress that lead to open heart surgery. It also led me to become sometime to a bit abrasive, and overly judgmental. Recognizing my humanity, and the struggles of all humanity helped me to wake up to the realization that I am not the sin police. I needed to spend more time sharing the love of Jesus and allowing the Holy Spirit to convict and change the lives of people. I also realized that my struggles were at times self-imposed, trying to be what I perceived others expected me to be. I remember in seminary days, my friends would call me "puritan Walter." It is not that I have never committed a sin, but I would remind people of lifestyles that were against the Word of God. When we focus so much on sin, we missed the joy of the Lord. I was good at "THOU SHALT NOT." However, I was not so good as what one should do.

I remember my wife saying to me one day, "You are so holy you have forgotten how to have fun." It was because I was so busy trying to get it right, that I kept missing the mark. In my quest to get it right, I really messed things up.

In their life's journey these prophets and kings were had real struggles in life. From Joseph to Paul these stories reflect my journey and struggles of life. What stories remind you that you are not complete, and that you need to seek to honor God everyday of your life?

I am learning my brokenness allows God to step in and be present in my life. My brokenness is knowing that I do not have full control, but I must submit to the will of God. My brokenness reminds me that I must rely on God. I am not suggesting using brokenness as an excuse to live recklessly, but I am saying a life without God is empty. My struggles may not be yours, but we all have struggles. We must learn to recognize the life lessons as result of our struggles. We are here on earth for a reason and a purpose. No, I am not the best that I can be, but I am a work in progress. I believe like Paul, I striving every day to live the life that Jesus has called me to live. (Philippians 3:14)

In my brokenness I am seeking to be a better servant for God, a better husband, a better son, a better father, a better pastor, a better friend, a better uncle, a better brother, and a better me. I also realize in my brokenness there is no shame in being me. My brokenness reminds me that I have not achieve what God has destined for my life. My brokenness keeps me hungry to know God even more, to have a better relationship with God, and display the love of God in my relationship with humanity.

We are trying to change to please the world and others, but our goal should be to please God. I know in pleasing God, I will become better for to do ministry, to share my faith, to live a godly life. It is not that I am perfect, but I recognize that I fall short in many ways. However, because of my relationship with God, He equips me to overcome where I fall short, and to live the life He desire for me to live. Submitting to God's will for my life, is realizing that I must allow Him to be in charge, and guide me through this journey. I am not complete or perfect, but I am trying every day, and I am becoming better. I pray that in your journey of faith, and life that you will surrender your life to God and that He may help you become a better you.

Reflection Questions

1. Becoming perfect will allow me to be_____?

2. Recognizing that you are not perfect has allowed you to

    _____?

3. In knowing that you will fail and has failed at things within

    your life makes you?

4. How do you work through your short falls, and failures that

    have occurred in your life?

Dear God

I ask that you guide me through the broken phases of my life. Help me God to grow, learn, and develop into a better person for your kingdom. God please open my heart to hear your voice, and to seek your face. God help to recognize that in the midst of all my struggles you are preparing me to live a life that is a reflection of your glory. Lord I pray that I may be a blessing to all people that you bring into my life.

In Jesus name.
Amen

References

All scripture in this book are from The Holy Bible, New Century Version of the Bible. HarperCollins Publishers. Nashville, TN 2005

Collins, Jim, *From Good to Great* Harper Business, 2001

Hill, Napoleon, *Think and Grow Rich*. Dover Publishing 2018

Marianne Williamson, A Return To Love: Reflections on the Principles of A Course in Miracles.

About The Author

Walter J. Green is a native of New Orleans, LA. He now lives with his wife and daughters in Memphis, TN where he pastors Friendship Baptist Church. He is also the Academic Dean of Tennessee School of Religion, a small Bible College in Memphis, TN. His life's motto is taken from Star Trek, "To boldly go where no man has gone before.

Rev. Dr. Green is a graduate of Memphis Theological Seminary where he earned the Doctorate in Ministry (2007). He received the Masters of Divinity Degree from United Theological Seminary in Dayton, Ohio (1994) and the Bachelor of Science in Mathematics from Southern University in New Orleans, LA (1991).

Other books by PBM Press

Meeting Space: One-On-One With God [Prayer Journal]
Hezekiah Loves Music: A Sacred Adventure
Hezekiah Loves Music: Learning Rhythms The Food Way
No Longer Afraid: Breaking Free of the Fear That Has You Bound
Angels Encamped About Me: Provision In The Wilderness
Gospel Songs Your Choir Will Love To Sing
Anthology of Art Songs and Spirituals By Contemporary African American Composers

All books are avaible at online book distributors such as Amazon
or are available directly by ordering on the following website:
https://revdonc.wordpress.com/bookstore